Cut It Out

Cut It Out

TEN SIMPLE STEPS FOR TIGHT WRITING AND BETTER SENTENCES

Laura Swart

*With original artwork
by Martin Wriglesworth*

Brush Education Inc.
www.brusheducation.ca

contact@brusheducation.ca

Copy editing: Leslie Vermeer
Cover design: Dean Pickup
Interior design and layout: Carol Dragich, Dragich Design

Library and Archives Canada Cataloguing in Publication

Swart, Laura, 1963–, author

    Cut it out : ten simple steps for tight writing and better sentences / Laura Swart with original artwork by Martin Wriglesworth.

Issued in print and electronic formats.

ISBN 978-1-55059-758-5 (softcover).—ISBN 978-1-55059-759-2 (PDF).— ISBN 978-1-55059-760-8 (Kindle).—ISBN 978-1-55059-761-5 (EPUB)

    1. English language—Sentences—Textbooks. 2. English language— Rhetoric—Textbooks. 3. Textbooks. I. Title.

PE1441.S93 2018   808'.042   C2018-900958-6
                                          C2018-900959-4

We acknowledge the support of the Government of Canada
Nous reconnaissons l'appui du gouvernement du Canada | Canadä

To Anika and Peter

Thank you

Brush Team, for your professionalism, dedication, and expertise; Leslie Vermeer, for your grace, intellect, and passion for our profession.

Alyssa Veck, Christine Dang, Janaina Spady, Danielle Hartung, and Jo-Anne Andre for showing me the manuscript through your eyes.

Martin Wriglesworth, for sharing your gift.

Mike Humphries, for making it happen.

Lonnie Graham, for making it beautiful.

Jeff, for standing beside me in sickness and in health.

Anika and Peter, for enriching my days.

Adonai, my joy, my peace, my sanctuary.

Contents

Introduction

Have you ever slumped over an essay and blurted out one of the following?

- I don't care what a gerund is! I just want a better mark on my next assignment!
- My writing is abysmal. But I have four classes, a part-time job, and a Bernese mountain dog to care for. I don't have a lot of time!
- I loathe grammar sites and grammar handbooks. They're boring and impossible to navigate.
- English is my second language, and I can't find my mistakes. English verb tenses are crazy!

If so, then read on. You'll learn how to write powerful, concise sentences without becoming a technician of English grammar. You'll obliterate excesses, creating openings to delineate your weighty ideas. And most importantly, you'll humour your professors by submitting intelligible essays and assignments.

How to Use This Book

You've probably heard it said that writing is 1 percent inspiration and 99 percent perspiration. I don't completely agree with that ratio; writing is in many ways a transcendent affair. But certainly, you will not improve with the wave of a hand. You must do the time. You must learn how to *see*—how to imitate, as Hans-Georg Gadamer defines it: understanding *essence*. You must discover who you are as a writer.

In this book, I've outlined ten common sentence errors that perhaps have caused your grades to dip below the surface. I begin each chapter by stating—and violating—one of the rules. Then, I give a sample of deplorable writing that you and I together will repair.

As you read, you'll find bolded terms that are defined in the glossary; each term is given both a colloquial and a conventional definition.

There is no answer key at the end of the book; writing isn't about right and wrong. There are rules, certainly—but then there is instinct. There are landmarks. And the landmarks, like Inukshuks, will guide you through an often-barren landscape and invite you into a larger narrative that is always evolving, always unfolding.

CHAPTER 1

Manitoba Resurrection

strings of little words

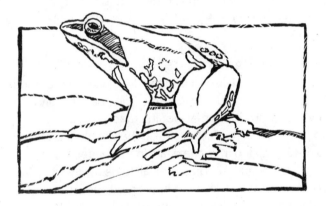

RULE #1

Try not to use too many strings of little words because
they really do add a lot of unnecessary clutter to your
sentences.

Have you ever met someone who rants on and on and on but
never says anything? Imagine what it's like to grade a paper that
does the same thing. I can assure you, your professor would rather
scrub toilets than read an essay that chatters like a magpie.

In rule #1, I used a strong word: *clutter*. But because it straggles behind a string of little words, it's invisible.

Strings are inventories of abstraction: *try not to use too many; they really do add a lot.* None of these words stirs the senses—the reader can't see them or hear them, so she must work harder to unpack the sentence.

To improve the sentence, I can say something like this: *Strings of little words clutter your sentences.* Now the two interesting words come into view: *strings* and *clutter*.

Why, you ask, is cutting out a few little words such a big deal? Think about it. If you cut two words from every sentence of a ten-page essay, you eliminate about 250 excesses—and make more room for the content-rich words and phrases that intoxicate your professors.

Sample Reading

There is a tiny little wood frog that lives deep in the woods of Manitoba. The truth is, this little frog doesn't really have any special attributes that would attract us to it, except for one small thing. Each spring, unbelievably, it is said to be resurrected from the dead. In the winter, when the outside temperatures drop and fall to below freezing, it doesn't choose to bury itself in the mud and it doesn't settle beneath the ice on the bottom of a frozen lake. Instead of this, it pretty much freezes to death in a hole in the ground. The wood frog's heartbeat and breathing slow down and after a period of time come to a stop. The water in its body very slowly crystallizes, and around 65 percent of it turns into ice. Its body temperature drops to a chilly −1 °C to −6 °C, and the frog becomes as hard and fragile as a piece of glass. Then, when the winter begins its long process of thawing out, the frog too begins to thaw—but it thaws from the inside out, not from the outside in, as a lot of people would expect.

My Corrections

Step 1

I first want to cut out the unnecessary words. Reread the first two sentences, and pay attention to the words in bold.

> There is a **tiny little** wood frog that lives deep in the woods of Manitoba. **The truth is,** this **little** frog doesn't **really** have any special attributes **that would attract us to it**, except for one small thing. Each spring, **unbelievably, it is said to be** resurrected from the dead.

I can improve these sentences by cutting the following words:

- *tiny*—means the same thing as little
- *the truth is*—redundant: the context indicates that I am relating facts, not fiction
- *really*—is this word really necessary?
- *that would attract us to it*—states the obvious; special attributes typically attract our attention
- *unbelievably, it is said to be*—dilutes the most important idea: resurrection from the dead

The sentences now read like this:

> There is a little wood frog that lives deep in the woods of Manitoba. This frog doesn't have any special attributes except for one small thing. Each spring, it is resurrected from the dead.

Before I move on, I want to ensure that the sentences are clear; sometimes when you cut out extra words, errors pop up out of nowhere. In the example above, I deleted the phrase *that would attract us to it*, but I forgot to insert a comma after *special attributes*.

> This frog doesn't have any special attributes, except for one small thing. Each spring, it is resurrected from the dead.

Step 2

Next, I'll underline the content-rich words—those that convey meaning—to see if I've overlooked any unnecessary little words.

> There is a little <u>wood frog</u> that <u>lives</u> deep in the <u>woods</u> of <u>Manitoba</u>. This frog <u>doesn't have</u> any <u>special attributes</u>, <u>except</u> for one small thing. <u>Each spring</u>, it is <u>resurrected from the dead</u>.

If I juggle a few things around, I'll have an impressive sentence:

> Deep in the Manitoba wood lives the common wood frog—a mundane little frog, apart from a singular eccentricity: each spring, it is resurrected from the dead.

Notice that I cut out **empty words** like *there*, *that*, and *this*. I used the **sensory words** *deep* and *dead* to empower the beginning and end of the sentence, and I inserted a **colon** (:) to highlight the frog's defining feature: its resurrection from the dead.

The original word count in step 1 is 50; the final word count is 27. The rewrite says the same thing more concisely—and, I think, more powerfully.

Step 3

Read the next few sentences of the paragraph.

> **In the** winter, **when the outside temperatures drop and fall to below freezing, it doesn't choose to** bury itself **in** the mud and **it doesn't** settle **beneath the ice on** the bottom **of** a frozen lake. Instead **of this,** it **pretty much** freezes to death **in** a hole **in** the ground. The wood frog's heartbeat and breathing slow down and **after a period of time come to a** stop. The water **in** its body **very slowly** crystallizes, and **around 65 percent of it turns** into ice. Its body temperature drops to **a chilly** −1 °C to −6 °C, and the frog becomes as hard and fragile as **a piece of** glass.

Once again, I'll cut out unnecessary words. Notice that wordy sentences usually contain too many **prepositions** (words like *on, in, beneath, to, from,* and *against*—they show relationships between ideas, people, and things). Here's a helpful hint: if a sentence has more than one or two of the prepositions *of* or *for* (I like to call them F-bombs), it probably needs a makeover. For example, you've perhaps read sentences like this in some of your textbooks: *It is the opinion of most experts that the consumption of too many foods comprised of high levels of saturated fats poses a health risk to individuals with a history of heart disease.* I don't feel like unpacking the entire sentence right now, but look at the phrase *the consumption of.* Why not just say *consuming* too many *saturated fats*? Why the pompous suffix (*-tion*)? Keep your words and sentences clean.

In corrected form, the sentences look like this:

> When winter approaches, it neither burrows into
> the mud nor settles on the bottom of a frozen lake.
> Instead, it retreats into a hole in the ground. It freezes
> virtually to death. When outside temperatures fall
> to below freezing, the wood frog's heartbeat and
> breathing slow down and finally stop. Its body
> temperature drops to between −1 °C and −6 °C. Over
> half of its bodily liquids crystallize into ice. The frog
> becomes as hard and fragile as glass.

I deleted the dead words, but the piece sounds rather dull, don't you think?

Step 4

Sometimes when you cut strings of little words, your piece turns into a cacophony of choppy little sentences. But think of the great songs you listen to: each one has balance, rhythm, and soul. Great writing is the same; it combines long, luxurious sentences with occasional bursts of clipped staccato—short, punchy sentences that give the reader a rest or add emphasis.

In the following rewrite, I used punctuation and **conjunctions** (*and, but, or, nor, yet, so, for*) to connect the choppy little sentences, and I changed a few other things that were irritating me:

> When winter approaches, it doesn't burrow into the mud or settle on the bottom of a frozen pond; it retreats into a hole in the ground **and** essentially freezes to death. As outside temperatures fall, the wood frog's heartbeat and breathing slow down to a stop, its body temperature drops to between −1 °C and −6 °C, and over half of its bodily liquids crystallize: **the** frog becomes as hard and fragile as glass.

The word count in step 3 is 109, and in step 4, it's 72. Not bad, eh?

Your Turn

Try to edit the final sentence of the paragraph. Cut out all unnecessary words and check for errors.

> Then, when the winter begins its long process of thawing out, the frog too begins to thaw—but it thaws from the inside out, not from the outside in, as a lot of people would expect.

CHAPTER 2

Okanagan Icewine
weak verbs

RULE #2
Weak verbs have always been a snare for writers, so it
would be best to use them judiciously.

A weak verb is any form of the structure "I am." You can adjust the
subject (*you* are; *I* am), the number (*they* are; *he* is), or the tense
(she *was*; they *have been*). One way to recognize weak verbs is to
look for *i* words, *h* words, and *w* words: forms of *is*, *have*, and *will*.

Don't snuff out all weak verbs with reckless abandon; they are, in fact, the scaffolds of English syntax. But do keep them in check, or you'll find them skulking around your sentences like stray cats. In rule #2, I can eliminate several words by saying, **Weak verbs are a snare for writers, so use them judiciously.** Or I can cut out the weak verb *are* and say, **Weak verbs dilute meaning, so use them judiciously.**

Sample Reading

You may have always wondered what good Canadian winters are if you have never been interested in skating or building snowmen. But in the Okanagan Valley, a treasure has been residing—a sumptuous little treasure that can only be found where the winters are cold enough: icewine.

Icewine grapes are produced from grapes that have been left on the vine until the first major frost has come. When the temperature has fallen below −8 °C, they will get as hard as a rock and will acquire just the right amount of sugar and flavour. While they are still frozen, they are picked by hand and pressed, and the water will come out in crystals of ice. What remains after that is a sweet, aromatic nectar. Then the grapes will have to ferment over a period of many weeks, and after that they will be aged in barrels for a few months, after which the wine will have become a lovely golden colour.

So the next time you are cursing the Canadian winter, have a sip of icewine. You will find that it is refreshing and sweet, and it will warm your temperament.

My Corrections

Step 1

Reread the first sentence.

> You may **have** always wondered what good Canadian winters are if you **have** never been interested in skating or building snowmen.

Check out the *h-words*. Each one inhabits a string of little words: *may have always; have never been*. Sometimes the h-word is useful, as in this sentence: *I don't want to go snowboarding with you tomorrow. I have never snowboarded in my life, and I don't want to crush my tailbone.* In this example, I used the h-word because it denotes the speaker's entire life—his past and present.

In my icewine example, however, the h-words bury the best parts of the sentence. Try to stick with the **simple present** and **simple past tenses** (typically verbs ending in *s* and *ed*, respectively) instead of using h- and w-words. When I cut the h-words from the above sentence, it looks like this:

> You may be wondering what good Canadian winters **are** if you **are** not interested in skating or building snowmen.

Step 2

The sentence now exists in the present, so it seems more—well, present—more real. But it still has two weak verbs, and when I add the next sentence, weak verbs and strings of little words begin to multiply like rabbits:

> You **may be wondering** what good Canadian winters **are** if you **are not interested in** skating or building snowmen. But in the Okanagan Valley, a treasure **has been residing**—a sumptuous little treasure **that can only be** found where the winters **are** cold enough: icewine.

Most of these weak verbs have to go.

> You may question the merits of Canadian winters if you don't like skating, tobogganing, and building snowmen. But in the Okanagan Valley, a treasure resides—a sumptuous little treasure found only where winters are cold: icewine.

I filled in the extra spaces with stronger words such as *merits* and *tobogganing* and still reduced the word count by ten. But the piece is a little flat, don't you think? I'll try again:

> Canadian winters are bleak and long if you don't skate, ski, or snowshoe, and if you're unacquainted with the Okanagan's sweet antidote—icewine— you'll barely survive.

Canadian winters strengthens the beginning of the sentence, and **dashes** showcase my topic, *icewine*. A few weak verbs have crept back into the piece, but I think they soften it.

Step 3

Read the next few sentences.

> Icewine **grapes are** produced from **grapes** that **have been** left on the vine until after the first **major** frost **has come.** When the temperature **has fallen** below −8 °C, they **will** get **as hard as a rock** and **will** acquire **just the right amount of** sugar and flavour. **While they are still** frozen, **they are** picked by hand and pressed, and the water **will come out** in **crystals of ice.** What remains after that **is** a sweet, aromatic nectar.

Because the h- and w-words are inessential to meaning, I want to rearrange the sentences and eliminate them:

> Icewine grapes remain on the vine until the first deep frost. When the temperature falls below −8 °C, they

> harden into little bullets of sweetness and flavour.
> Harvesters pick the frozen grapes by hand and press
> them, extracting the water in ice crystals. The juice
> then settles into a golden, aromatic nectar.

I put human beings—harvesters—into the sentence to cut out passive (weak) verbs (I'll address the passive voice in chapter 3), and I strengthened the beginning and end of each sentence. I also changed the word *major*, which is a little informal, to *deep*. Notice that two of the verbs, *falls* and *settles*, now have an *s*.

Your Turn

Edit the final sentences, and focus on the w-words. Don't miss the string of little words in the last sentence.

> Then the grapes will have to ferment over a period
> of many weeks, and after that they will be aged in
> barrels for a few months, after which the wine will
> have become a lovely golden colour.

> So the next time you are cursing the Canadian winter,
> have a sip of icewine. You will find that it is refreshing
> and sweet, and it will warm your temperament.

CHAPTER 3

New Brunswick Fiddleheads

passive voice

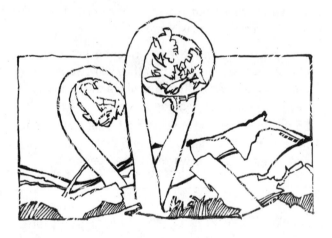

RULE #3

Passive voice should not be used by writers.

The passive voice reminds me of a little kid caught in a lie: she talks in circles and trips over her words. In rule #3, the agent (*writers*) appears after the verb (*used*). Another version of the passive voice in this sentence is *the passive voice should not be used.* Here, the sentence abandons the agent altogether.

Passive voice is particularly loathed by English professors because it is characterized by strings of little words. (Did you catch the passive voice in that last sentence?) Rule #3 is more direct when I say, **Writers should not use the passive voice.** But remember that writing is more about essence than rules; if the passive voice works well in a sentence, use it.

Sample Reading

The delight of fiddleheads is not in their sumptuous taste or their voluptuous crunch; it is in their enigma. Fiddleheads are also known as *croziers*, alluding to the curved staff used by shepherds. Just as the sheep are guarded by the shepherd, fiddleheads are jealously guarded by the foragers who search for them. And for good reason—in New Brunswick, at least, they are an ethereal delicacy.

They come out each spring around the banks of rivers and streams, but in a few weeks when the tightly coiled shoots begin to unravel, they become bitter and inedible. They are finicky little things, too. They must be eaten the same day they are purchased, or their flavour diminishes and they spoil. And they must be boiled for just the right amount of time; if overcooked, they turn into slimy green muck.

Fiddleheads can be served simply with butter and seasoning, but they can also be sautéed with bacon and garlic or preserved in a lemon marinade, making them crisp and full of flavour. For a more assertive flavour, a Dijon-tarragon sauce can be added, or a shrimp, fiddlehead, mushroom medley in a light thyme sauce can be tossed together. If nurtured carefully, their eccentric flavour will be coveted by any palate.

My Corrections

Step 1

The passive voice is sometimes difficult to detect. Look for clues: the words *be* and *by* are often lurking around. Read the phrase below:

> Just as the sheep are **guarded by** the shepherd

In a passive sentence, the person or thing that makes the action happen is called the *agent* and is signalled by the word *by*. I want the agent—the shepherd who guards the sheep—to be my subject:

> Just as a shepherd guards his sheep

Here, I cut out the word *by* and placed the subject (*shepherd*) before the verb (*guards*).

Step 2

The following phrase reveals a slightly different problem, an absent subject:

> They must **be eaten** the same day they **are purchased,** or their flavour diminishes and they spoil.

Who is eating and purchasing the fiddleheads? We don't know; the doer of the action is absent. I need to insert a subject:

> Their flavour expires quickly; they begin to spoil as soon as they leave the market.

By making fiddlehead *flavour* the subject of the first part, I cut out the word *be*; in the second part, fiddleheads (*they*) are the subject.

Step 3

The next phrase is also missing a subject:

> And they must **be boiled** for just the right amount of time; if overcooked, they turn into slimy green muck.

Remember, the subject is the person or thing doing the action. This phrase doesn't indicate who is boiling the fiddleheads. I can rewrite it as follows:

> And if you overcook them, they become slimy green muck.

Notice that I suddenly introduced the **second-person point of view** (*you*). Don't make shifts like this part way through a piece of writing. And because the second-person is colloquial (see chapter 6) and unrefined, it might make your professor's hackles rise. I'll try something else:

> And overcooking turns them into slimy green muck.

Step 4

Find the passive voice in the next phrase:

> Fiddleheads can be served simply with butter or oil and seasoning, but they can also be sautéed with bacon and garlic or preserved in a lemon marinade, making them crisp and full of flavour.

Now determine how I eliminated the passive voice:

> Some people dress their fiddleheads plainly with oil and seasoning; others prefer a fusion of flavours, sautéing them with bacon, garlic, and mushrooms or preserving them in a fresh lemon marinade.

Here, I inserted the subject *some people* and reduced the word count by two. Notice, however, that I shifted the emphasis from *fiddleheads* to *some people*. If I want to highlight the fiddleheads, I need to keep the passive voice.

Your Turn

Edit the final sentence for passive voice. First find the verb; then determine whether the doer of the action is present. Look for *by* and forms of *be*, possible signs that the passive voice is being used. (Any passive voice in that last sentence?)

> For a more assertive flavour, a Dijon-tarragon sauce can be added, or a shrimp, fiddlehead, mushroom medley in a light thyme sauce can be tossed together. If nurtured carefully, their eccentric flavour will be coveted by any palate.

CHAPTER 4

Halifax Gateway
progressive tense

RULE #4
Don't try using the progressive tense unless the context
of your piece is asking for it.

The progressive tense is an action word with an *ing* attachment.
Some sentences require the progressive tense, as in, *Beatrice is eating her pickled herring right now, and the whole room is beginning to stink.*

But unless something is happening *right now* or over a period of time, use the **simple present** and **simple past** tenses (typically verbs ending in *s* and *ed*, respectively); they are neat and tidy and they don't make your professor's head throb.

Rule #4 is easy to revise: **Don't use the progressive tense unless the context of your piece requires it.**

Sample Reading

I'm standing in the reception area of Pier 21—renovated now, reopened. And I'm thinking back to the day in 1948 when I arrived at the Halifax waterfront, Canada's gateway to freedom. Trying to escape my war-torn country, I had come to Canada to find a new life. I was carrying only a small suitcase containing a pair of trousers, two pairs of socks, a Bible, and some crumpled photographs. Everything else I left behind.

I remember stumbling from the boat and feeling the cool wind snapping at my face. Watching the seagulls swooping, I was smelling the salty air and feeling the sprays of water gusting off the sea.

Walking into Pier 21, I dumped my suitcase onto the mounds of other baggage, stretching out on the unyielding wooden floor, trying to get some sleep. But even though I was feeling physically exhausted, I was wide awake for hours, feeling desperately homesick and alone. And I was afraid, wondering how likely it was that I would be able to make it in this new country.

Today, as I am looking around at the new Pier 21, I'm thinking that I too have been refurbished by my decades in Canada, stripped and rebuilt like an antique armoire. But I'm feeling unsettled. I'm shifting and turning like an Atlantic wind, still trying to find a place to touch down.

My Corrections

Step 1

Check out the sentences that begin with *ing* words. In each example, more than one thing is happening at once.

> **Trying** to escape my war-torn country, I had come in 1948 to find a new life.

In this sentence, the progressive tense (*–ing*) is acceptable; in coming to Canada, the narrator was *trying* to escape war.

Step 2

The next example, however, doesn't quite work:

> **Watching** the seagulls swooping, I was **smelling** the salty air and **feeling** the sprays of water gusting off the sea.

Here, the progressive tense is downright annoying. Was the narrator watching the seagulls, smelling the air, and feeling the water all at the same time? And if he was, do you even care?

The sentence also highlights peripheral words like *watching*, *smelling*, and *feeling* instead of the more interesting nouns and verbs—seagulls swooping and water gusting. The following rewrite, I think, is better:

> I can still see the seagulls swooping; I can smell the salty air gusting off the sea.

Step 3

Read the next sentence.

> **Walking** into Pier 21, I dumped my suitcase onto the mounds of other baggage, **stretching** out on the unyielding wooden floor, **trying** to get some sleep.

The progressive tense in this sentence is, well, a bit of a lie. It's unlikely that the narrator threw his baggage on the pile exactly when he walked through the door and stretched out on the floor; he probably walked through the door first, then threw his bag down, then stretched out on the floor.

Here is an improved version:

> I plodded into Pier 21, dumped my suitcase onto the mounds of other baggage, and stretched out on the unyielding wooden floor to get some sleep.

Step 4

Now look at some other progressive tense constructions:

> I'm **standing** in the reception area of Pier 21— renovated now, reopened. And I'm **thinking** back to the day in 1948 when I arrived at the Halifax waterfront, Canada's gateway to freedom. **Trying** to escape my war-torn country, I had come to Canada to find a new life.

The first two examples, *standing* and *thinking*, are in my view effective. They bring the piece into the present: it's happening here and now. I could have used the **simple present tense** (I *stand*; I *think*), but the progressive tense implies that the narrator is lingering; even the sound of -*ing* lingers on your tongue.

The problem is that I have three *ing* words in quick succession: *standing, thinking, trying*. Instead, I want the sentences to read something like this:

> I'm standing in the reception area of Pier 21— renovated now, reopened. And I'm thinking back to the day in 1948 when I arrived at the Halifax waterfront, Canada's gateway to freedom. I had come to Canada to escape—war, poverty, affliction—to find a new life.

Step 5

Read the next few sentences of the paragraph.

I was **carrying** only a small suitcase with a pair of trousers, two pairs of socks, a Bible, and some crumpled photographs. Everything else I left behind. I remember **stumbling** from the boat **and feeling the cool wind snapping at my face. I can still see the** seagulls **swooping**; I can smell the salty air **gusting** off the sea.

I think the following rewrite is better. Do you agree?

I had only a small suitcase with a pair of trousers, two pairs of socks, a Bible, and some crumpled photographs. Everything else I left behind. I remember stumbling from the boat: gusts of salty wind snapped at my face and grey gulls hung heavy in the air, suspended like marionettes.

I cut the annoying little words and changed the seagull sentence again, but I'm still not satisfied. I might return to this section later.

Your Turn

Edit the remaining sentences for the progressive tense. Remember, you probably don't want to cut out every -*ing*. The bolded sentence is exasperating because—you guessed it—it's loaded with insipid little words.

But even though I was feeling physically exhausted, I was wide awake for hours, feeling desperately homesick and alone. **And I was afraid, wondering how likely it was that I would be able to make it in this new country.**

Today, as I am looking around at the new Pier 21, I'm thinking that I too have been refurbished by my decades in Canada, stripped and rebuilt like an antique armoire. But I'm feeling unsettled. I'm shifting and turning like an Atlantic wind, still trying to find a place to touch down.

CHAPTER 5

Yukon Lights

repetition

RULE #5

Do not, absolutely *do not,* repeat words and phrases in
sentences and paragraphs unless they are keywords and
phrases in the sentences and paragraphs or unless you
are trying to achieve a certain effect in your sentences
and paragraphs.

Repetition is sometimes necessary or poignant, but most nouns, adjectives, and verbs should tread only once into a paragraph, and if they are powerful words, into an entire paper.

The exception, of course, are keywords. If you're comparing, say, children and basset hounds, you must repeat the words *children* and *basset hounds* throughout the paper. The moment you insert synonyms such as *offspring* or *canines*, your reader begins to vibrate.

I can edit rule #5 by saying, **Do not repeat words and phrases within paragraphs unless you want to achieve a certain effect or unless they are keywords and phrases.** I repeated the word *unless* for effect; I want to emphasize the important exceptions to the rule. In addition, I repeated *words and phrases* for clarity.

Sample Reading

When Yukon nights are long and dark, and when winter thins out into spring, aurora borealis sweeps across the horizon—the Dance of the Spirits, the Cree call it. This amazing spectacle occurs when the sun releases energy-charged dust particles that plunge into Earth's atmosphere. When the dust particles gather into a cloud, it is known as a plasma, and a stream of plasma is known as a solar wind. The solar wind takes two to five days to reach the earth's atmosphere. When the solar wind strikes the gases in Earth's magnetic field, the particles make different gases start to glow in different colours, depending on which gases are struck and how far the gases are from Earth. When the particles in solar winds strike oxygen atoms, the colour red becomes visible. When the particles strike nitrogen molecules, the colour pink becomes visible. Nearer to Earth, the oxygen atoms will produce shades of green, and nitrogen molecules produce shades of blue and violet.

But I think something more is involved, as the Cree describe it. This amazing spectacle cannot be bracketed by quantitative data. I think something else is at play, something that overcomes us and draws us in, so that we do not remain what we were, so that we do not remain the same.

My Corrections

Step 1

I wanted to begin the piece with some mystery, just as aurora borealis is mysterious, so I repeated the word *when* for artistic effect and to delay the opening data.

Step 2

The words *amazing spectacle* in the second sentence have no **sensory** appeal: I can't see, hear, smell, taste, or touch them, so I'll cut them out.

> When Yukon nights are long and dark, and when winter thins out into spring, aurora borealis sweeps across the horizon. This *Dance of the Spirits*, as the Cree call it, occurs when the sun releases energy-charged dust particles that plunge into Earth's atmosphere.

Step 3

Read the following sentences and underline the repeated words.

> This *Dance of the Spirits*, as the Cree call it, occurs when the sun releases energy-charged dust particles that plunge into Earth's atmosphere. When the dust particles gather into a cloud, it is known as a plasma, and a stream of plasma is known as a solar wind. The solar wind takes two to five days to reach Earth's atmosphere. When the solar wind strikes the gases

> in Earth's magnetic field, the particles make different
> gases start to glow in different colours, depending
> on which gases are struck and how far the gases are
> from Earth.

I repeated *dust particles*, *plasma*, and *solar wind* twice in three sentences. Although they are keywords, the reader doesn't want to see them again and again and again and again, so I'll combine a few sentences and cut out the repetition.

> This *Dance of the Spirits*, as the Cree call it, occurs
> when the sun releases energy-charged dust particles
> that plunge into the earth's atmosphere and **gather
> into a plasma. A stream of plasma, or solar wind,**
> reaches the atmosphere in two to five days and
> strikes the **gases** in the magnetic field, making **them**
> glow in different colours, depending on which **gases**
> are struck and how far **they** are from Earth.

I cut out the word *gases* twice by inserting the **pronouns** *them* and *they*. I also exchanged *Earth* for *the earth* to fine-tune the sentence without using a wacky synonym. Don't lose your lunch over this—it's better to repeat yourself than to confuse your reader.

Step 4

Rather than draw you into a complex discussion about English syntax—which I'm certain would enthrall you, but which I don't have the stomach for right now—I'll simply draw your attention to the commas in the piece. (By the way, what do you think of my repetition of *which* and *draw* in the previous sentence—good, bad, or ugly?) Notice that the first draft has four commas and no other punctuation except periods:

> This amazing spectacle occurs when the sun releases
> energy-charged dust particles that plunge into
> Earth's atmosphere. When the dust particles gather
> into a cloud, it is known as a plasma, and a stream of

plasma is known as a solar wind. The solar wind takes two to five days to reach Earth's atmosphere. When the solar wind strikes the gases in Earth's magnetic field, the particles make different gases start to glow in different colours, depending on which gases are struck and how far the gases are from Earth.

Below, I used six commas and three **conjunctions** to combine sentences, creating a more interesting and complex read:

This *Dance of the Spirits*, as the Cree call it, occurs when the sun releases energy-charged dust particles that plunge into the earth's atmosphere **and** gather into a plasma. A stream of plasma, **or** solar wind, reaches the atmosphere in two to five days **and** strikes the gases in the magnetic field, making them glow in different colours, depending on which gases are struck and how far they are from Earth.

Step 5

Don't forget about rules #2 and #3: weak verbs and passive voice. The second sentence repeats the weak verb *are*:

making them glow in different colours, depending on which gases **are** struck and how far they **are** from Earth.

If you're thinking that the first *are* looks suspiciously like the passive voice, you're probably awake. I'll rewrite the phrase as follows:

making them glow in different colours, depending on the types of gases and their proximity to Earth.

Step 6

Read the next section.

When the **particles** in solar winds **strike** oxygen atoms, the colour red **becomes visible**. When the

particles strike nitrogen molecules, the colour pink **becomes visible.**

Have you ever heard of **parallelism**? Parallelism involves balancing parts of a sentence to add beauty or clarity. I'll give it a try in the form *when x strikes y*:

When the solar winds strike oxygen atoms, dark reds illuminate the sky; **when they strike** nitrogen molecules, brilliant pinks begin to glimmer.

I repeated the words *when* and *strike* for clarity and inserted the **pronoun** *they*. I replaced *becomes visible* with the verbs *illuminate* and *glimmer* to cut out repetition. But writing is about layering, and I don't like the feel of this new sentence. I want to make it more artful. What do you think of the following revision?

When the solar winds strike oxygen atoms, dark reds soak up the sky; when they strike nitrogen molecules, the reds succumb to pinks.

Notice my use of the **semicolon** (;). Semicolons join sentences (or *independent clauses*, for you jargon junkies) that are closely related—like twin brothers.

You wouldn't use a semicolon in the following sentence because the independent clauses aren't related: *For breakfast this morning, I had pancakes with whipped cream, chocolate chips, cherries, and syrup; I'm going swimming now.* However, if you create a conceptual link between pancakes and swimming, you can use a semicolon:

For breakfast this morning, I had pancakes with whipped cream, chocolate chips, cherries, and syrup; I'm going swimming now, and I think I'm going to puke in the pool.

Step 7

I now have a problem with the word *when*. *When* isn't a keyword, but I used it twice in the first sentence. Notice how many *when*'s occur in the paragraph.

When Yukon nights are long and dark, and **when** winter thins out into spring, aurora borealis sweeps across the horizon. This *Dance of the Spirits*, as the Cree call it, occurs **when** the sun releases energy-charged dust particles that gather into a plasma and plunge toward Earth's atmosphere. A stream of plasma, or solar wind, reaches the atmosphere in two to five days and strikes the gases in the magnetic field, making them glow in different colours depending on the types of gases and their proximity to Earth. **When** the solar winds strike oxygen atoms, dark reds soak up the sky; **when** they strike nitrogen molecules, the reds fade into pinks.

Which is more important: the artistic effect in the first sentence or the **parallelism** in the final sentence? I prefer to keep the parallelism because it adds clarity. I want to cut one *when* from the first sentence and make a few changes to the second. See what you think.

When Yukon nights are long and dark and winter thins out into spring, mysterious sheets of light sweep across the horizon: the *Dance of the Spirits*, the Cree call it. The Dance begins when the sun releases energy-charged particles that gather into a plasma and plunge toward Earth's atmosphere.

You're probably mumbling about my repetition of *and* in the first sentence, but I'm trying to imply that things are happening over a long period of time. Nights and winters are long, just as the sentence is.

I'm now brooding over the six *the*'s. Maybe I'll return to this sentence later when I'm more alert. (By the way, why do you think I added the phrase *The Dance begins*?)

Now, notice the **colon** (:) in the first sentence. A colon means *stop and look: the next part is important.* I use **dashes** (—) in the same way, but with a dash, the second part is kind of a sidekick—like a kid sister. Do you think I should use a colon or a dash after *sweep across the horizon*?

I use several dashes and at least one colon every time I write. Give them a try—you'll come off looking like a brainiac.

Your Turn

Read the final few sentences and try to cut the repetition (although you might decide to keep some of it for effect). Don't miss the w-word and the passive voice (see rules #2 and #3).

> Nearer to Earth, the oxygen atoms will produce shades of green, and nitrogen molecules produce shades of blue and violet.
>
> But I think something more is involved, as the Cree describe it. This amazing spectacle cannot be bracketed by quantitative data. I think something else is at play, something that overcomes us and draws us in, so that we do not remain what we were, so that we do not remain the same.

CHAPTER 6

Canmore Sisters
colloquial language

RULE #6

Avoid colloquial language like the plague; it's *so* not cool in academic writing.

Rule #6 is totally in your face. I usually come across more subtle colloquialisms in student writing. Colloquial language is okay in email exchanges, story writing, and books like *Cut It Out*, but in academic essay writing, if you've heard it said before, don't say it again. I can rewrite rule #6 like this: **Colloquial language is inappropriate in academic writing.**

Sample Reading

The *Three Sisters* near Canmore, Alberta are known individually as *Big Sister, Middle Sister,* and *Little Sister,* or *Faith, Hope,* and *Charity.* They were first named *The Three Nuns* by Albert Rogers in 1883: "There had been quite a heavy snow storm in the night, and when we got up in the morning and looked out of the tent, I noticed each of the three peaks had a heavy veil of snow on the north side, and I said to the boys, 'Look at the three nuns.'" To Rogers, the peaks looked like three praying nuns. And believe me, you better say a prayer or two if you want to summit the Three Sisters.

Big Sister is—you guessed it—the highest of the three siblings; it's a good scramble beginning on the south side. You'll start in the trees, but after the treeline breaks, you'll get to walk the ridge toward the top. Very cool. You'll see a couple of interesting rock formations, which you have to go around before summiting. Because of steep snow patches near the top in the early season, wait until late June or July before you head out.

Middle Sister is a long scramble from Stewart Creek, and like a middle child, it is often overlooked. There's really nothing definitive about it; it's just an insanely long hike. But the wild flowers, birds, mountain sheep, deer, and other wildlife make the trek a real good one. When you hit the summit, you'll definitely want to chill for awhile and enjoy the epic views.

True to her name, Little Sister is like a rotten little kid that can't be reasoned with. Little Sister is a tough climb requiring technical climbing skills. Avoid the scree on the ascent and hike up the ridge, although the slab terrain on the ridge is no picnic, either. The biggest nightmare is the final traverse up a steep slope toward the summit. Bring an ice ax and crampons in the early season in case there is snow. Come to think of it, don't go at all in the early season unless you're an experienced climber—or you may take a tumble to death. Take the scree on the way down, but watch out: more than one climber has been nailed by falling rock.

Here's a few cautionary words for you if you decide to climb the Three Sisters. Bring tons of layers and a windbreaker for the summit, which can get nasty, even on a hot July day. Don't forget lunch, water, sweets, and a camera to capture those views. And remember, the Three Sisters are in grizzly country. Bring bear spray and make noise. Let's bring 'em back alive.

My Corrections

Step 1

In some ways, I enjoy this piece because it has a strong **voice**. I can picture the speaker: she's an experienced climber in her late twenties, her lip and tragus are pierced, and she never parts with her wool socks or fleece jacket.

But the writing event is a trinity of sorts: writer, audience, and text—so don't lose sight of **audience** and **purpose**. If you're writing the piece as a guide for hikers and climbers, you should try to *encourage* them to go into the mountains—not unnerve them with the lore of rockslides and carnivorous animals. One of your first tasks as a writer, then, is to determine who your audience is and shape your piece accordingly.

Step 2

I need to distinguish between **jargon** and **colloquial language**. Jargon is the specialized language of a particular group or activity.

In this piece, words such as *scramble, summiting, scree, slab terrain,* and *traverse* are examples of jargon. A reader unfamiliar with climbing may not understand their denotations, but because hikers are my intended audience, I don't need to define them. Keep this in mind when you write your next political science essay. Don't include Webster's definitions of *collectivism* or *Marxism* unless you believe Webster has insights into socialism that your professor lacks.

Colloquialisms are everyday words and expressions; they should not appear in academic writing. However, if a direct quotation contains a colloquialism, I can't cut it out:

"and I said to the boys, 'Look at the three nuns.'"

Albert Rogers is speaking to men, not boys, but I want to keep the quotation intact; the colloquialism conveys something of the relationship between the men.

Step 3

Read the following sentence.

And believe me, **you** better say a prayer or two if **you** want to summit the Three Sisters.

If I'm writing a guidebook for climbers, the phrases *believe me* and *you better say a prayer or two* might work. But if I'm writing an essay about the Canadian Rockies, the sentence is way out of line. I want to keep the reference to prayer, however, because I find it intriguing. Maybe the sentence could read like this:

And I'm certain that some hikers have whispered a prayer or two before summiting one of the Sisters.

Notice that I cut out the **second-person point of view** (*you*), which you should avoid using in most academic writing assignments. Use the **third-person point of view** (*she, he, it, they*) instead; the third-person plural (*they*) is the easiest structure to work with. Many professors also accept the **first-person point of view** (*I, we*).

I also want to avoid **contractions** (*I'm*) because they're too informal, so I have to edit the sentence yet again:

> And I suspect that some hikers have whispered a prayer or two before summiting one of the Sisters.

Step 4

The following sentence contains a rather subtle colloquialism:

> Come to think of it, don't go at all in the early season unless you're an experienced climber—or you may take a tumble to death.

Come to think of it conveys the internal life of the writer, which is irrelevant outside of a personal reflection paper.

Take a tumble to death is pretty dramatic. I'll save it for my next murder mystery and instead say, *Only experienced climbers should go in the early season; others could be seriously injured.*

Your Turn

Try to find additional colloquialisms in the piece—words that are common in speech but inappropriate in academic writing.

CHAPTER 7

Prairie Sky
overloaded sentences

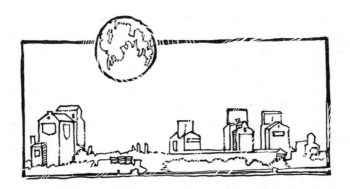

RULE #7

Rather than overloading your sentences with hordes of images, ideas, and grammatical scaffolding and in doing so, overwhelming your reader and sending her into mind-altering oblivion, there are several tools you can employ—tools such as parallelism, subordination, conjunctions, etc.—that will make your sentences much more enjoyable to read and that will avoid the pitfall many fall into of composing dull little sentences that sound like a five-year-old banging out *Mary Had a Little Lamb* on the piano.

C.S. Lewis once said that writing is like being in love: an idea grabs hold of you and won't let go. You become feverish; you crave words and phrases like a pregnant woman craves ice cream, like a chocoholic craves chocolate, like a speed demon craves speed. Ever had that problem?

Overwriting attacks students who are addicted to words. They pack their writing so full of pomposity that sentences begin to look like distended cows. But size doesn't matter in writing: power does.

Check out my rewrite of rule #7: **Rather than overload your writing with images, ideas, and grammatical scaffolding, use strategies such as parallelism, subordination, and conjunctions to construct balanced, rhythmic sentences.**

This rewrite, though more concise than the original, has stripped the sentence of its art: it has about as much rhythm as a bleating sheep. Why don't you return and edit it after reading this chapter? Depending on your **audience** and **purpose**, you might want to reinstall the five-year-old. But try to shake off the dubious word *etcetera*, or your reader might think that either you don't know what you're talking about or you're too uninspired to complete the sentence.

Sample Reading

I know why they call Saskatchewan the land of the living skies. I have seen the infinitely vast, brooding, naked blue Saskatchewan sky, provoked by dusk, unravel into a rage of swirling reds and purples. When I'm stretched out on the grass looking in fascination at that infinite canvas, I'm somehow plucked from my world—from my sterilized hall of mirrors—and yoked into something ongoing—something greater than I am. The Saskatchewan sky addresses me and interrogates me and challenges my convictions; it presses itself into me and defies me to describe it, to explain it. I can't help writing about it. Sometimes I'm stiff like a prairie wind, applying the words in singular, controlled flicks of thought; other times I fling words about in a frenzy, my paper inverting into a Pollock original. And I wonder. Do I own my work? Am I the sole proprietor of its meaning, or is meaning a collaborative construction, a bartered commodity? Does a piece of writing have a life of its own—is it living and active like a Saskatchewan sky, or is it a transmitter of a self-present truth, of a fixed referent? Is it essentially static and atomistic—an impotent social construction with a fixed horizon, an illusory limit with synthetic boundaries that occupy an artificial playing field, a society governed by standardized epistemologies? Yet the prairie sky has no borders. It cannot be confined or possessed; it can only be ventured into as it opens up and absorbs me and imposes itself upon me: something greater is present and emerging—something that extends beyond my control. It calls me into the questions of my existence; it asks something of me. No wonder blue is the colour of divinity.

My Corrections

Step 1

If your writing looks something like this, don't panic—even great writers like Michel Foucault write difficult, layered prose. Read the first few sentences again.

> I know why they call Saskatchewan the land of the living skies. I have seen the infinitely vast, brooding, naked blue Saskatchewan sky, provoked by dusk, unravel into a rage of swirling reds and purples. When I'm stretched out on the grass looking in fascination at that infinite canvas, I'm somehow plucked from my world—from my sterilized hall of mirrors—and

> yoked into something ongoing—something greater
> than I am. The Saskatchewan sky addresses me and
> interrogates me and challenges my convictions; it
> presses itself into me and defies me to describe it, to
> explain it.

I like the opening sentence because it invites the reader to explore the Saskatchewan sky. But the second sentence uses too many adjectives to describe that sky. The reader has to absorb *infinite, vast, brooding, naked, Saskatchewan,* and *blue* in a split second, so every word loses power. Never use more than one or (in rare cases) two adjectives to complement a noun, even if the adjectives are evocative, artistic, indelible, and profound.

The same rule applies to other parts of a sentence, such as verbs and adverbs (*ly* words). It's better to say *she devoured her liver and onions* than *she ate her liver and onions quickly and hungrily.* If you choose a strong verb in the first place, adverbs invariably water it down. (Do I need the adverb *invariably?*)

I want to choose the most powerful adjectives, and for now, I'll keep the phrase *Saskatchewan sky* because I like the **alliteration**— the juxtaposition of similar sounds to magnify meaning.

Now I'll delete one more adjective from the list: *infinite, vast, brooding, naked,* and *blue. Infinite* and *vast* are similar in meaning, so I'll cut *vast* because I prefer the rhythm of *infinite.*

The sentences now convey three essential ideas: the sky is really big; the sky, like a person, has moods; and the sky is naked—it reveals something.

I'm going to cut out *infinite* because the piece later talks about boundlessness, and I don't want to repeat myself. I like *brooding,* but *naked* is more consistent with the main idea that the sky is living and active and *revealing.*

Here are my revisions:

> I know why they call Saskatchewan the land of the
> living skies. I have seen the naked blue Saskatchewan

> sky, provoked by dusk, unravel into a rage of swirling
> reds and purples.

I still have three adjectives—*naked, blue, Saskatchewan*—to describe the noun *sky*, and the sentence is a bit wordy. My final revision looks like this:

> I know why they call Saskatchewan the land of the
> living skies. I've seen its naked blues unravel into a
> rage of reds and purples.

What do you think? I moved the **alliteration** from *Saskatchewan sky* to *rage of reds*, and I cut out the repetition of *Saskatchewan* (see rule #5). I added the contraction *I've* because I wanted to change the beat of the sentence. Because the piece is written as a narrative in the **first-person point of view**, it doesn't require the level of formality that an academic essay does (see rule #6).

Step 2

Read the next sentence.

> I know why they call Saskatchewan the land of the
> living skies. I've seen its naked blues unravel into a
> rage of reds and purples. And when I'm stretched
> out on the grass looking in fascination at that infinite
> canvas, I'm somehow plucked from my world—
> from my sterilized hall of mirrors—and yoked into
> something ongoing—something greater than I am.

I don't like the part about stretching out on the grass, and I've heard the sky referred to as a canvas before (see rule #6). Here are my changes:

> I know why they call Saskatchewan the land of the
> living skies: when I see its naked blues unravel into
> a rage of reds and purples, I'm plucked from my
> sterilized hall of mirrors and yoked into something
> ongoing, something greater than I am.

I changed the punctuation several times before writing this version, and I kept the repetition of *something* because it threads something mythical into the piece. But I might take out the *hall of mirrors*; it's a little over the top.

The next two sentences are also a bit zealous.

> The Saskatchewan sky addresses me and interrogates me and challenges my convictions; it presses itself into me and defies me to describe it, to explain it. I can't help writing about it.

I like the idea of the sky *addressing* me; it's a subtle invitation to ponder the mystery of creation. The words *interrogate* and *challenge*, though interesting, decrease the power of the phrase by two-thirds, so I have to cut them. Writers call these types of words *little darlings*: they are enchanting words that we are forced to part with in the interest of preserving our reader's well-being.

I now want to combine my ideas into one sentence:

> The Saskatchewan sky addresses me; it presses itself into me and summons me to write.

Notice that the phrase *it presses itself into me* is **sensory**; you can almost feel the weight of the sky.

Step 3

Read the next few sentences.

> Sometimes I'm stiff like a prairie wind, applying the words in singular, controlled flicks of thought; other times I fling words about in a frenzy, my paper inverting into a Pollock original. And I wonder. Do I own my work? Am I the sole proprietor of its meaning, or is meaning a collaborative construction, a bartered commodity? Does a piece of writing have a life of its own—is it living and active like a Saskatchewan sky, or is it a transmitter of a self-present truth, of a fixed referent? Is it essentially static

and atomistic—an impotent social construction
with a fixed horizon, an illusory limit with synthetic
boundaries that occupy an artificial playing field, a
society governed by standardized epistemologies?

I like the first sentence because it **alludes** to Jackson Pollock, whose work embodies inner life through movement, colour, and design—like a Saskatchewan sky does. **Allusion** carries with it another world, deepening the writing event.

The next part asks two questions relative to Pollock: *Who determines what meaning is? Is meaning alive or static?* I can't develop two enormous ideas like this in one short piece, so I'll put aside the question of who owns my work and focus on whether or not meaning changes like a Saskatchewan sky does. My rewrite looks like this:

Sometimes I'm stiff like a prairie wind, applying
the words in singular, controlled flicks of thought;
other times I fling words about in a frenzy, my paper
inverting into a Pollock original. And I wonder. Does
a piece of writing have a life of its own? Is it living
and active like a Saskatchewan sky, or is it essentially
static and atomistic, an impotent social construction?
Is it boundless, or does it have a fixed horizon—an
illusory limit, a synthetic boundary that occupies
an artificial playing field, a society governed by
standardized epistemologies?

This section looks pretty smart, but I have no idea what it means. And it asks the same thing twice: is writing dead or alive? I'll cut out another sentence and sharpen the question.

Sometimes I'm stiff like a prairie wind, applying
the words in singular, controlled flicks of thought;
other times I fling words about in a frenzy, my paper
inverting into a Pollock original. And I wonder. Is a
piece of writing living and active like a Saskatchewan

> sky, or is it a series of impotent metaphors that are,
> in Nietzsche's words, worn out and without sensuous
> power?

Nietzsche's *worn-out metaphors* create a powerful image in a few words, and the essential question now is, does my writing breathe and expand, or does it recycle worn-out ideas? You might ask the same question of your own writing.

Your Turn

Rewrite the final sentences, and try to convey the same content in half the words. Notice the passive voice in the second sentence (see rule #3). Do you think it's necessary?

> Yet the prairie sky has no borders. It cannot be
> confined or possessed; it can only be ventured into as
> it opens up and absorbs me and imposes itself upon
> me: something greater is present and emerging—
> something that extends beyond my control. It
> calls me into the questions of my existence; it asks
> something of me. No wonder blue is the colour of
> divinity.

CHAPTER 8

Montreal Bagels

choppy little sentences

RULE #8

Avoid choppy little sentences. They all sound the same.
They put readers to sleep.

Sometimes making cuts leaves a residue of choppy little sentences that are about as interesting as the ring around your bathtub. I can improve rule #8 by blending the three sentences: **Choppy little sentences marching in succession put readers to sleep.**

I combined the sentences by cutting the **pronoun** *they*. The image of *marching*, I hope, conveys the idea of noisy little sentences banging down one after the other. The only problem is that banging doesn't put people to sleep, and the sentence feels a little inflated, a little overwritten (see chapter 7). Perhaps I should link the sentences together with punctuation and a **conjunction** (*and*): **Avoid choppy little sentences: they all sound the same, and they put readers to sleep.** It has a nice rhythm, don't you think?

Sample Reading

I smell the aroma of baking bread. It makes me weak. It's coming from the bagel shop. I look inside. A man is tossing dough in the air. He kneads it and he tosses it up again. It's yielding. A hole is forming in the middle. He lines up the unbaked bagels and puts them in a wood-fired kiln. They come out singed.

I go inside. There's multigrain, whole wheat, blueberry, sesame seed, flax seed, poppy seed, cream cheese, strawberry jam, and smoked salmon. I have to choose. I have to fill that hole in the middle.

My Corrections

Step 1

All of these sentences have a simple structure—someone or something is doing something. Look at the first four sentences: *I smell, it makes, it's coming, I look.* These sentences could use some rhythm, so I think I'll link them together:

> The aroma of bread baking makes me weak (mon Dieu!), so I press my face against the glass and look inside.

I cut out *I smell* because it's redundant; if I'm weak from the aroma, then I must be smelling something. I also used a **conjunction** (*so*) to show a cause–effect relationship between the two ideas: because the smell is so good, I look inside.

I think the phrase *I press my face against the glass* is more interesting than *I look inside*. Good writing is in the details; it's in **sensory words** that I can see, feel, hear, smell, and touch—not in snotty academic language.

I changed the order of *baking bread* to *bread baking* because my voice inflects more when I say the words aloud. Sound always adds depth—ask any musician. Writing is more about following instincts than strategies, so go with your gut.

Step 2

Read the next few sentences.

> A man is tossing dough in the air. He kneads it and he tosses it up again. It's yielding. A hole is forming in the middle.

These sentences get the job done—barely. I want to develop the relationship between the man and the dough, and this, I hope, will knead the ideas together.

> A man is tossing dough high in the air; over and over he's tossing, and the dough keeps falling into his ubiquitous hands. He kneads it and he reasons with it and he tosses it up again. And it's yielding: a hole is forming in the middle.

Does this version seem more meaningful to you? I gave the dough a resistant nature: the man must work with it and reason with it before it will yield. There is a progression of thought here, not just a recounting of facts.

In the first sentence, I used three *ing* words (*tossing, tossing, falling*) to imply that the dough is yielding over time (see rule #4). In the second sentence, I repeated *he* and *it* to achieve the same effect.

I also tossed in a few interesting words. *Ubiquitous* implies that the man's hands are everywhere; he's careful with the dough and he's in control. *Reasons* and *yielding* show relationship, connectedness.

The **semicolon** (;) and **colon** (:) bring ideas together: the semicolon unites twin brothers and the colon, a mother and daughter.

Step 3

This piece is sounding like a free verse poem, so I'll assign a line to each idea.

> the aroma of bread baking makes me weak (mon Dieu!)
> i press my face against the glass and look inside
> a man is tossing dough high in the air
> over and over he's tossing, and the dough keeps falling
> into his ubiquitous hands
> he kneads it and he reasons with it
> and he tosses it up again
> and it's yielding
> a hole is forming in the middle

I want to divide the poem into three main ideas or stanzas. Notice the difference between the first rewritten stanza and the final two stanzas.

> the aroma of bread baking makes me weak (mon Dieu!)
> i press my face against the glass and look inside
> a man is tossing dough high in the air
> over and over he's tossing, and the dough keeps falling
> into his ubiquitous hands
> he kneads it and he reasons with it
> and he tosses it up again
> and it's yielding
> a hole is forming in the middle
>
> He lines up the unbaked bagels.
> He puts them in a wood-fired kiln.
> They come out singed.

I go inside.
There's multigrain, whole wheat, blueberry,
sesame seed, flax seed, poppy seed,
cream cheese, strawberry jam, and smoked salmon.
I have to choose.
I have to fill that hole in the middle.

Your Turn

Try to rewrite the final two stanzas. Add **sensory** words and small details to connect ideas; then use **semicolons, colons,** and **conjunctions** to connect sentences. If you're uncomfortable with poetry, edit the paragraph below the poem.

He lines up the unbaked bagels.
He puts them in a wood-fired kiln.
They come out singed.

I go inside.
There's multigrain, whole wheat, blueberry,
sesame seed, flax seed, poppy seed,
cream cheese, strawberry jam, and smoked salmon.
I have to choose.
I have to fill that hole in the middle.

OR ...

He lines up the unbaked bagels and puts them in a
wood-fired kiln. They come out singed. I go inside.
There's multigrain, whole wheat, blueberry, sesame
seed, flax seed, poppy seed, cream cheese, strawberry
jam, and smoked salmon. I have to choose. I have to
fill that hole in the middle.

CHAPTER 9

Niagara Daredevils

uncontrolled sentences

RULE #9

Every uncontrolled sentence is incomprehensible and indeed reprehensible because it goes on and on and on and never allows the reader to come up for air or to pause and reflect on what the sentence means, so the reader is really just holding her breath and waiting to

> get to the end to return to the beginning again to try to decipher what the thing is saying, so all I ask is that you try to find a way to break it off.

Nothing loses an audience faster than an uncontrolled sentence (your high school teacher might have called it a *run-on sentence*). Think *skipping record*: all you want to do is hit the thing. Your professors feel the same way, but instead of wading through your piece, they tell you to keep sentences short, and sometimes even prescribe the number of words that a sentence should have.

But how many notes are in a song? How many spices are in a soup?

Notice that rule #9 is probably error free, but it's difficult to follow—not because it's too long, but because it's imbalanced.

I can improve the sentence and keep it intact by adding punctuation and making a few small changes: **Every uncontrolled sentence is incomprehensible—reprehensible, even—because it goes on and on and never allows the reader to come up for air, as it were—it never allows her to pause and ponder the meaning; instead, she holds her breath and waits for the end so she can return to the beginning, start again, and try to decipher what the thing is saying. So I ask you: find a way to break it off.**

If you're uneasy about the length of the sentence, I'll break it up for you: **Every uncontrolled sentence is incomprehensible—reprehensible, even—because it goes on and on and never allows the reader to come up for air, as it were; it never allows him to pause and ponder the meaning. Instead, he holds his breath and waits for the end so he can return to the beginning, start again, and try to decipher what the thing is saying. So I ask you: find a way to break it off.**

Sample Reading

The Niagara Falls have lured more than one adventurer seeking fame and fortune; some achieved their goals, others died trying, and Annie Edson Taylor falls somewhere in the middle. On October 24, 1901, at 63 years old, with stockings and slippers, her lucky heart-shaped pillow, and a mythical black kitten, she climbed into a custom-made oak-and-iron pickle barrel weighted with a 200-pound anvil to keep it balanced and a small mattress to cushion her body, and she fastened herself into a leather harness and prepared for the ride of her life. After securing the lid, friends pressurized the chamber of the barrel with a bicycle pump, plugged the hole with a cork, and pushed Annie into the wild Niagara currents one mile from the Canadian Horseshoe Falls, at the bottom of which photographers, tourists, and Annie's manager, whom she had hired to publicize the event, watched as the barrel, pulled by the strong current, whirled toward the roaring falls and over the precipice behind the wall of mist. Eighteen minutes later, Annie was pulled out of her barrel alive and relatively well, but she was badly shaken and exclaimed that no one should ever attempt such a feat, especially since it did not award the dividends that she had hoped for because she only earned a small amount of money speaking about her experience and posing for photographs, but was never able to achieve her dream of gaining fame and fortune and died in poverty at age 83.

My Corrections

Step 1

I want to cut out the first sentence and begin in the middle—or *in medias res*—to spare you the preview and get right to the show. Writers often cut the first two or three sentences of a first draft.

That's okay: sometimes we need to roam around for a while before we get to the good stuff—kind of like a road trip.

Step 2

Read the next sentence. I put *Annie Edson Taylor* near the beginning and *Niagara Falls* at the end to add clarity.

On October 24, 1901, at 63 years old, with stockings and slippers, her lucky heart-shaped pillow, and a mythical black kitten, Annie Edson Taylor climbed into a custom-made oak-and-iron pickle barrel weighted with a 200-pound anvil to keep it balanced and a small mattress to cushion her body, and she fastened herself into a leather harness and prepared for the ride of her life: over the Niagara Falls.

This sentence is error free, but it makes your head hurt because it packs in too many random details: the date, Annie's age, the slippers, the pillow, the cat, the anvil, the mattress, the harness, and the ride. Details are pivotal to powerful writing, but don't forget what your mom taught you: all things in moderation.

So first, I'll juggle a few things around:

On October 24, 1901, Annie Edson Taylor climbed into a custom-made oak-and-iron pickle barrel weighted with a 200-pound anvil to keep it balanced and a small mattress to cushion her body. With stockings and slippers, her lucky heart-shaped pillow, and a mythical black kitten, she fastened herself into the leather harness and prepared for the ride of her life: over the Niagara Falls. She was 63 years old.

The little sentence at the end reveals Annie's age and hints at her reckless behaviour. Close to the beginning is the main action—climbing into the barrel—and inside the barrel we find Annie holding her cat, fastening herself in, and preparing herself mentally.

Step 3

The string of adjectives (*custom-made, oak-and-iron pickle*) helping the noun (*barrel*) is a mouthful. If you can't get your tongue around it, your reader probably can't stomach it—and besides, adjectives drain the power of nouns (see rule #7).

I want to keep the adjectives that strengthen my main idea: Annie is a risk-taker, and that's a big deal. So I'll focus on the skimpy pickle barrel:

> On October 24, 1901, Annie Edson Taylor climbed into a wooden pickle barrel

There are still too many facts clogging the piece. I can stir up some emotion by changing a few words (mostly verbs).

> On October 24, 1901, Annie Edson Taylor **squeezed** into a wooden pickle barrel **weighted with a** 200-pound anvil to keep it balanced **and a** small mattress to cushion her body. **Clutching** her heart-shaped pillow and **squirming** black kitten, she fastened herself into the leather harness, **stared into the darkness,** and prepared for the ride of her life: over the Niagara Falls. She was 63 years old.

Each new word conveys the idea that Annie is in a threatening situation.

The phrase *weighted with* applies to two things: the anvil and the mattress. But the mattress serves to protect Annie's body, not to balance the barrel. To fix the problem, I need to change the wording:

> On October 24, 1901, Annie Edson Taylor squeezed into a wooden pickle barrel **outfitted with** a 200-pound anvil for balance and a small mattress to cushion her body.

Step 4

The next sentence goes on and on and on like a physics lecture. But don't be fooled: long sentences are glorious, like long walks on the beach. Try to find the problem—and by the way, the sentence is error free.

> **After** fastening the lid, friends pressurized the chamber **of the** barrel **with a** bicycle pump, plugged the hole **with a** cork, and pushed Annie into the wild Niagara currents one mile from the Canadian Horseshoe Falls, **at the bottom of which** photographers, tourists, and Annie's manager, **whom she had** hired to publicize the event, watched **as the** barrel, pulled by the strong current, whirled toward the roaring falls **and over the** precipice behind the wall of mist.

To me, nothing stands out in this sentence. Good writing moves up and down like Annie's barrel drifting toward the Falls. Some sentences are heavily weighted; others provide relief.

My rewrite looks like this:

> Friends fastened the lid, pressurized the chamber, corked the hole—and pushed Annie into the wild Niagara River. The strong currents hurled Annie's barrel over the thundering falls and into the heavy mist. At the bottom, photographers and tourists waited.

The word count changes from 77 to 40. Notice the bolded little words (rule #1) that I cut from this draft. Writing, like all art, is about making choices—deciding what to keep and what to leave behind.

Your Turn

Edit the final sentences on your own. Keep a few potent details, and cut out the useless little words.

> Seventeen minutes later, Annie was pulled out of her barrel alive and relatively well, but she was badly shaken and exclaimed that no one should ever attempt such a feat, especially since it did not award the dividends that she had hoped for because she only earned a small amount of money speaking about her experience and posing for photographs, but was never able to achieve her dream of gaining fame and fortune and died in poverty at age 83.

CHAPTER 10

Arctic Inukshuks

fragments

RULE #10

Fragments. Some say they're errors. Because they're
incomplete. Others use them for stylistic effect. Although
students should handle them with care.

A fragment is a piece of something; it's incomplete, like a Happy
Meal without a toy. Sometimes writers use fragments deliberately
for effect, but for now, let's assume that they're bad news and cut
them all out.

The first sentence of rule #10 has a subject (*fragments*), but it doesn't say anything about the subject. Some writers use this type of fragment for effect, but it's kind of corny, don't you think?

The next sentence is complete; it has a subject (*some*), and it tells us what the subject is doing (*saying something*).

Did your junior high teacher foam at the mouth every time you began a sentence with *because*? His agitation, it turns out, was partially justified. Some sentences (not all) that begin with *because* are incomplete because they're missing one of the two parts: the cause or the effect.

Similarly, the phrase *Although students should handle them with care* is also missing its better half. You often hear sentences like this in conversation, but talking and tweeting and texting are as far removed from academic writing as cow liver is from *foie gras*.

Sometimes you can fix a fragment by fusing it with the sentence before or after it. I'll correct rule #10, then, as follows: **Some say fragments are errors because they're incomplete, others use them for stylistic effect—although students should handle them with care.**

Because the two parts of the sentence are related, I connected them with a comma. But do you see the error? Never use a comma by itself to join two sentences (independent clauses), or you'll have a **comma splice** on your hands. Instead, use a **semicolon** (;) or a comma with a **conjunction**.

The sentence should read like this: **Some say fragments are errors because they're incomplete; others use them for stylistic effect—although students should handle them with care.**

I used a **dash** (—) at the end because this part is an appendage, or a dog's tail, if you will. Go crazy with punctuation—you'll have a blast. Just remember, a **colon** joins a mother and daughter: one side is more powerful than the other; a **semicolon** joins twin brothers—but a **dash** merely joins a teenager with her kid sister. Note, however, that a dash is still more powerful than a comma—it highlights important information.

Sample Reading

The tundra of the Canadian Arctic. White, governed by permafrost, few landmarks save the Inukshuks. Each a unique creation built from piles of stones that show the way. The Inuit use Inukshuks as navigational markers on a stark landscape with changing features of ice and snow. Inukshuks point out dangerous places, good hunting and fishing, caches of food, and migration routes of caribou. They also manifest Inuit spirituality. Indicating locations of death and of where spirits abide. As emblems of community life. They mark where decisions are made and where celebrations are held. Intimate to Inuit culture; they are compelling in that they mediate the past and the present. Bringing to presence another reality. They are contemporary, yet they are something repeated. A remnant of the past. They are a narrative always unfolding. A summons of Inuit history and culture.

My Corrections

Step 1

Read the first two sentences again.

> The tundra of the Canadian Arctic. White, governed by permafrost, few landmarks save the Inukshuks.

The first sentence is missing a verb, and the second is missing a subject. So it seems logical to join them.

> The tundra of the Canadian Arctic is white and governed by permafrost, with few landmarks save the Inukshuks.

Step 2

The sentence is now grammatically correct, but it's a little drab. I'll spice it up by emphasizing one part of it.

> The Canadian Arctic is governed by permafrost, not people, and the Inukshuks—the only true landmarks—show the way.

Here I alluded to the primacy of the natural environment in the North. I used **dashes** to set apart an important idea—that the Inukshuks govern this environment in a way that no federal or territorial government could. I want to build on this idea throughout the piece.

Don't miss the red flag *by*, possible evidence that the passive voice is nearby (rule #3). I can flip the phrase to cut out the passive voice.

> Permafrost—not people—governs the Canadian Arctic, and the Inukshuks, the only true landmarks, show the way.

Which version of the sentence do you prefer?

Step 3

Read the next few sentences.

> Each a unique creation built from piles of stones. The Inuit use Inukshuks as navigational markers on a stark landscape with changing features of ice and snow. Inukshuks point out dangerous places, good hunting and fishing, caches of food, and migration routes of caribou. They also manifest Inuit spirituality. Indicating locations of death and of where spirits abide.

Can you spot the fragments? The first sentence is missing a verb. You might argue that *built* is a verb, but the main verb should accompany the subject (the who or what) of the sentence. This sentence refers to *each* inukshuk, right? But the verb *built* applies to *unique creation*. So the subject *each* needs a verb:

Each is a unique creation built from piles of stones.

Step 4

The last sentence is also a fragment. Watch out for sentences that begin with -*ing*; they often need two parts, like *because* and *although* sentences. I can correct this fragment by attaching it to the previous sentence.

They also manifest Inuit spirituality, indicating locations of death and of where spirits abide.

Your Turn

The final sentences of the piece are miserable: most are short fragments, a semicolon is incorrect, the repetition is pointless, and little words are piling up like Saturday chores. Review rules #1 to #9 and make improvements.

As emblems of community life. They mark where decisions are made and where celebrations are held. Intimate to Inuit culture; they are compelling in that they mediate the past and the present. Bringing to presence another reality. A remnant from the past. They are contemporary, yet they are something repeated. They are a narrative always unfolding.

A summons of Inuit history and culture.

Conclusion

You made it! You're now writing powerful sentences, concise sentences, sentences with beauty and rhythm and depth. You're learning to cut out excesses—and eliminating errors in the process. Your grades are leapfrogging to the Northern lights, as it were. So what now? Well, in Paul Cezanne's words, you will astonish Paris. Not with an apple—but with a sentence.

Glossary

alliteration: stuttering on paper
  (aka the juxtaposition of similar sounds to magnify meaning)

allusion: seeing stuff that's not there
  (aka an indirect reference)

audience: the poor sap who has to read your writing
  (aka the readership of a written text)

colloquial language: stuff you say to your peeps but not to your priest
  (aka language used in ordinary conversation)

colon: part of the large intestine
  (aka the mark of punctuation that separates mother–daughter clauses, the second of which develops or illustrates the first)

comma splice: a fraudulent comma
  (aka two independent clauses joined by a single comma, which is too weak to do the job)

conjunction: part of a song you learned in grade school
  (aka a word that joins other words, phrases, and sentences—in particular, and, but, or, nor, yet, so, for)

contraction: too lazy to write the whole word
  (aka the shortened version of a word, with omitted letters replaced by an apostrophe; examples are I'm, couldn't, and you're)

dash: a short race
  (aka the mark of punctuation that appends a phrase or an idea to an existing sentence—like a sidekick or a kid sister)

empty words: words with no soul
  (aka words that do not appeal to the senses)

first-person point of view: it's all about me
  (aka writing from the perspective of the speaker using I or we)

in medias res: on-campus living quarters
  (aka "into the middle of things": the tactic of opening a piece in the middle of a narrative or plot)

jargon: stuff you say to your priest but not to your peeps
  (aka the specialized language of a particular group or activity)

parallelism: something you failed on your driving test
  (aka deliberately repeating part of a sentence to add beauty or clarity)

preposition: a little word that gets under your skin
  (aka a word that shows relationships between ideas, people, and things—for example, on, in, beneath, to, from, and against)

pronoun: a fake noun
  (aka a word that stands in the place of a noun, such as you, me, something, or nothing)

purpose: your reason for living
  (aka the author's reason for writing a text)

second-person point of view: it's all about you
  (aka writing that addresses the reader using you)

semicolon: a mutated period
  (aka the mark of punctuation that joins closely related sentences)

sensory words: words that light your fire
  (aka words that appeal to the senses)

simple past tense: d-verbs
  (aka a verb that uses d or ed to describe something that happened before the present; it is not supported by an auxiliary verb)

simple present tense: s-verbs
  (aka a verb that ends with an s to describe something that is happening right now; it is not supported by an auxiliary verb)

third-person point of view: it's all about your friends
  (aka writing that discusses its subject using he, she, it, or they)

voice: you
  (aka specific choices in writing style that communicate information about the writer)

Inspirations

Chapter 1

Fox, Douglas. 1999. "Cold-Blooded Solutions to Warm-Blooded Problems." Accessed December 8, 2017. http://www.exploratorium.edu/frogs/woodfrog/index.html

North American Wood Frogs. Accessed December 8, 2017. http://www.youtube.com/watch?v=uRx_cl826Mo

Chapter 2

Canada Icewine Introduction. Accessed December 12, 2017. https://www.youtube.com/watch?v=-59RlSzQBfc

Ice Wine: Really Worth $250,000 for a Bottle? Accessed December 12, 2017. https://www.youtube.com/watch?v=5cNlSTmh4Sg

Chapter 3

Fiddleheads Steamed. Accessed December 8, 2017. https://www.youtube.com/watch?v=flk4yya41ig

Chapter 4

CBC. 2010. "Pier 21, Halifax, Nova Scotia." Accessed December 8, 2017. http://www.cbc.ca/sevenwonders/wonder_pier_21.html

Pier 21—Halifax, Nova Scotia—Gateway to Canada. Accessed December 8, 2017. http://www.youtube.com/watch?v=Nw3Z4MlLXHs

Chapter 5

NASA Video about Aurora Borealis. Accessed December 8, 2017. http://www.metacafe.com/watch/500268/nasa_video_about_the_aurora_borealis/

Northern Lights Centre. N.d. *Northern lights.* Accessed December 8, 2017. www.northernlightscentre.ca/northernlights.html

Chapter 6

Canmore—Three Sisters Sunrise. Accessed December 8, 2017. http://www.youtube.com/watch?v=A7yvcLsCPjI

Peakfinder. N.d. "The Three Sisters." Accessed December 8, 2017.
http://www.peakfinder.com/peakfinder.ASP?PeakName=the+three+sisters

Chapter 7

Land of the Living Skies—Saskatchewan, Canada. Accessed December 8, 2017.
http://www.youtube.com/watch?v=w4FhM-yPQd8

Chapter 8

Montreal vs New York Bagel Comparison—An Ancient Battle for Supremacy.
Accessed December 12, 2017. https://www.youtube.com/watch?v=IGlFhJe5TyU

Something You Should Eat: Montreal Bagels. Accessed December 12, 2017.
https://www.youtube.com/watch?v=rGqgNn5K_tg

Chapter 9

Annie Edson Taylor. Accessed December 8, 2017. http://en.wikipedia.org/wiki/
Annie_Edson_Taylor

Chapter 10

Pinnacle Farms. 2009. "The Inuksuk." Accessed December 8, 2017. http://www.
pinnaclefarms.ca/ORIANAsite/AboutNameandLogo/InuksukNew.html

About the Author

Laura Swart is passionate about writing and teaching. She taught academic writing at the University of Calgary for over twenty years, encouraging students to find and raise their writing voices. She is a published novelist and the Director of I-AM ESL, an English-language school that uses story and song to teach the intricacies of English to refugees. Laura lives in Calgary with her husband and two children.

About the Artist

Martin Wriglesworth grew up on the prairies of Alberta and now lives on the Sunshine Coast. He attended the Alberta College of Art and Design in the 1980s and is currently a pastor who enjoys being creative.